my australian library

At the Beach

Kathie Atkinson

A LITTLE ARK BOOK

ALLEN & UNWIN

Pipis

Pipis live just under the sand at the edge of the sea. If a wave uncovers them they can burrow down again in a moment. A pipi's shell has two halves, which can shut tightly to protect the soft body inside. The tubes you can see here are like straws for sucking in water and squirting it out.

Tritons

You can find tritons at low tide in rock pools. Some grow quite big, and have beautiful colours. Inside the tough shell is the triton's soft body which pokes out when it wants to eat or move about. Tritons and pipis are like the snails that live in your backyard.

Chiton

Chitons (say 'kite-ons') are also called coat-of-mail shells. On top they have strong plates of shell that overlap, like bits of armour, and protect the soft body underneath. Their colours blend in with the rocks where they live. They can move along like snails, or clamp on tightly.

Sea Urchin

A sea-urchin has a round shell covered in spines. Some have spines as thin and sharp as needles. This is a slate-pencil urchin which has spines about as thick as crayons. Sea-urchins move around on tiny tube-feet, with their mouths underneath their bodies. They eat mainly seaweed.

Anemone

An anemone looks like a sea-flower, but it is an animal. Its body is soft, with a mouth in the middle and tentacles around the top. The tentacles wave about in the water and trap bits of food. This is a green anemone, but you can find many other colours.

Jellyfish

This purple stinger has a soft, see-though body like a ballerina's skirt, with lacy tentacles that trail behind and catch small fish. It is covered in poison cells that can give you a sharp sting. Jellyfish are not really fish.

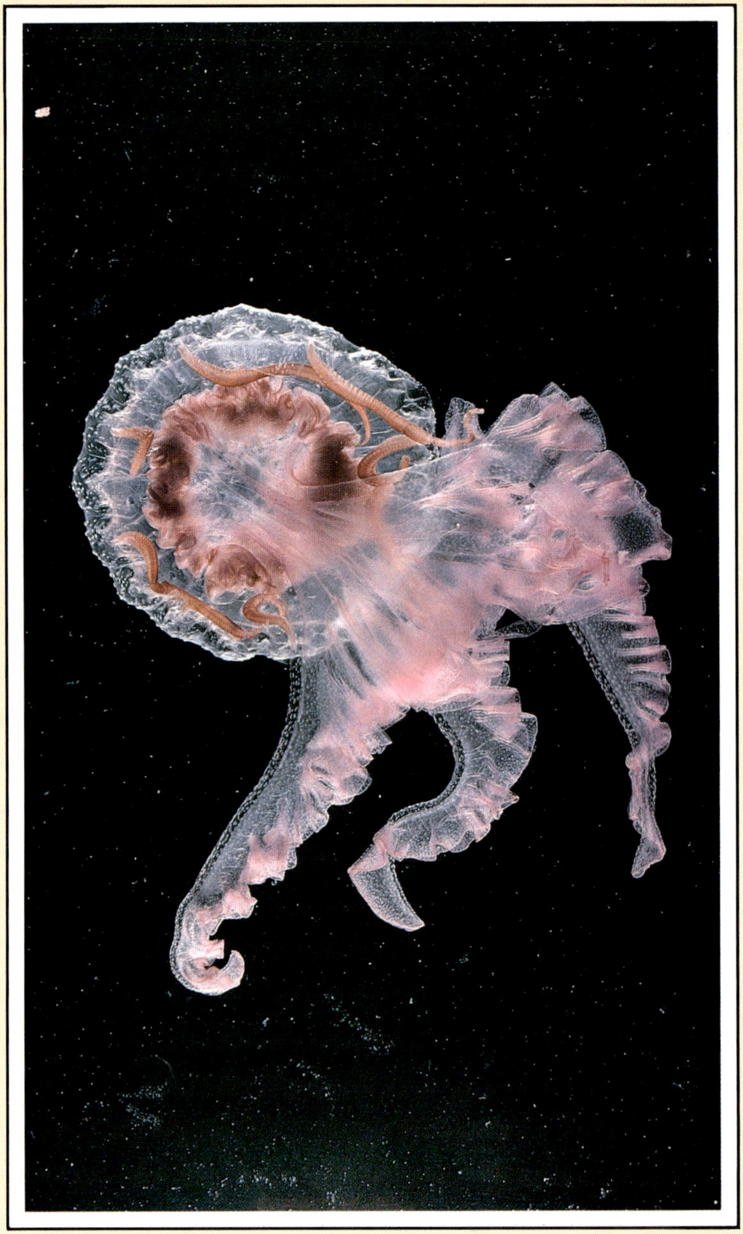

Bluebottles

These beautiful creatures have a small air sac that floats on the water, with a mass of blue tentacles hanging down below. The long tentacles are poisonous fishing-lines for catching small sea creatures. They can sting you very badly, even when they are washed up dead on the beach.

Crab

You can find crabs in holes in the sand and mud, under rocks, among mangroves, and in shallow water. They have a tough outer shell, ten legs, strong claws for catching food, antennae for feeling their way, and eyes which are sometimes on stalks. Most crabs scuttle sideways.

Hermit Crab

A hermit crab has a softer tail than most crabs, and makes its home in the shell of a dead sea-snail. It can move around nimbly with the shell on its back, and will hide inside when there is danger. As the crab grows, it has to find a bigger shell to live in.

Goose Barnacles

Bottles, driftwood, even old thongs that you find on the beach can be covered in goose barnacles. These barnacles have a soft stalk like a goose's long neck, with a hard part at the end, which protects their body. They spend their lives at sea, attached to a floating object, going where it goes.

Shark's Egg

This may not look like your idea of an egg, but it is the egg-case of a Port Jackson shark. Each case contains one large egg yolk, just as a hen's egg does. The mother shark fixes her eggs to weed or rock under the sea, but the eggs sometimes tear off and are washed ashore among the seaweed.

Toado

The toado, or toadfish, is a very common fish in rock pools and around jetties. You can catch one quite easily with a hand-line, but don't eat it, because it is poisonous. Its dappled skin helps it hide among seaweed, where it feeds on small shellfish and algae.

Eels

Eels are fish, but they have long, thin bodies, rather like snakes. They can grow as long as a tall man. These green moray eels lurk with their tails in a hole in the rock and their heads floating in the water. They catch small fish to eat, and sometimes bite divers with their sharp teeth.

Seahorse

A seahorse is a strangely-shaped fish, with a head that looks a bit like a horse's. It swims upright through the water, moving slowly, and curls its tail round bits of weed when it wants to stay still. The mother seahorse lays eggs into the father's pouch, and he carries them until they hatch.

Octopus

The common octopus lives in rock pools, changing colour to match its surroundings, and squeezing itself into small cracks to hide. It crawls along and grasps things with its eight long arms which are covered in suckers. It can swim jerkily by sucking in water and squirting it out.

Sea-stars

Sea-stars, or starfish, usually have five arms and are star-shaped, but some look more like footballs. There are many different coloured ones in rock pools and on reefs. They creep about slowly with their mouths underneath, eating coral, sponges and other small creatures. If they lose an arm, they can grow a new one.

Brittle-star

Brittle-stars are more slender and graceful than sea-stars, and often have beautiful patterns. They move fast, with each arm wriggling like a snake. The arms break off very easily, but can grow again. Brittle-stars hide under rocks, away from sunlight.

Coral

Corals grow in many shapes and colours. This is called staghorn coral because it looks like antlers. It is made of thousands of little animals called polyps. Each polyp has a hard outer skeleton and soft tentacles that can reach out to catch plankton floating in the sea.

Sponge

Sponges look like plants, but they are animals. They grow in the sea, fixed in one place, and suck water through their bodies to catch bits of food. They form colourful gardens for other animals, such as tiny shrimps, to live in. Your bath sponge may be a dead sponge from the sea, or a copy.

Seagulls

These seagulls are wheeling and diving for fish scraps in the wake of a fishing boat. They eat almost anything they can find, and gather on the beach, or around jetties and rubbish bins, to squabble over bits of food. They can float on water, but they build their nests on the ground.

Penguin

Fairy penguins are the smallest penguins in the world. They are not built to fly, but can swim very well with their torpedo-shaped bodies and strong flipper-wings. At dawn they swim out to sea to fish. At night they come ashore in groups and waddle up the beach to their burrows.

Shearwater

Shearwaters make nests and raise chicks in burrows in the ground near the beach. If you walk close by at night, in spring, you will hear the birds crooning and making sounds like people wailing. They spend time at sea, catching small fish and other animals, and fly in a lazy-looking way.